Haunted Houses **3**

The Midnight Children

PAMELA RUSHBY

Illustrated by Kevin Burgemeestre

Triple**3**Play

sundance™
A Haights Cross Communications Company

A Haights Cross Communications ✦® Company

Copyright © 2000 Sundance/Newbridge Educational Publishing, LLC

Published by
Sundance Publishing
P.O. Box 740
One Beeman Road
Northborough, MA 01532
800-343-8204

Copyright © text Pamela Rushby 1999
Copyright © illustrations Kevin Burgemeestre 1999

First published 1999 as Supa Dazzlers by
Addison Wesley Longman Australia Pty Limited
95 Coventry Street
South Melbourne 3205 Australia
Exclusive United States Distribution: Sundance Publishing

ISBN-13: 978-0-7608-4800-5
ISBN-10: 0-7608-4800-9

Printed in China

Contents

Chapter 1

Lights in the Night

"Andy, are you really sure you need all this?" said Mom. "You're only camping at the scout cabin for one night. How much stuff do you need?"

"I need all of it," said Andy. "Don't I, Isabel?"

I looked at the pile. "Well," I said. "Do you really think you'll need the boots? And the board game? And you know you can't take Sammy!"

"It might rain," said Andy. "And we need something to do after dinner. Sammy's not going. He just likes sitting on my sleeping bag."

Mom patted our new puppy, Sammy. "Well, whatever," she said. "I'm sure your scout leader won't mind if you bring a few extra things. But you're going to need help to get it all there, and Dad's got the car. We'll have to walk down with you. Where's Tom?"

Andy glanced at me. "He's at Jenna's," she replied. "He said he'd be back soon."

I didn't say anything. We'd only moved to this little town a few months ago—Mom and Dad; my brother Tom, who's sixteen; my sister Andy, who's nine; and me. I'm Isabel, and I'm thirteen. We met Jenna soon after we got here. She goes to high school with Tom.

I liked Jenna, but I didn't like the way she and Tom were getting along so well. I was feeling left out and lonely. I was trying not to show it, but I couldn't fool Andy.

"Here's Tom now," said Mom. "Oh, good, he's brought Jenna, too. They can both help."

"Great," I said.

We picked up Andy's stuff and set off down
the street. It was Mom, Tom, Jenna, me,
Andy, Sammy, and Alexander, Jenna's big
German shepherd. We were all—except for
the dogs, of course—carrying camping gear.
Good thing the scout cabin is only a couple
of streets away, I thought.

But then, nothing was too far away from anything else in this little town. We went down a street of big old houses with very big yards. My friend, Mr. Watling, lives on this street. Then we went down a street of small new houses, past the school, past a little wooden church, and there was the scout cabin.

Next to the scout cabin was another big old house. The house was set back from the street, and the whole yard was overgrown. "Interesting old place," said Mom. Mom likes old houses. "Who lives there, Jenna?"

"No one," said Jenna. "I can't remember anyone ever living there."

At the scout cabin, the whole troop of little girls was running in and out, and yelling. Brown Owl, their patient scout leader, was trying to calm them down.

"Best of luck," said Mom to Brown Owl.

"Will you get any sleep at all?"

Brown Owl laughed. "They'll be worn out by nine o'clock," she said.

Jenna grinned. "That's not how I remember scout camp," she said.

"Oh, you!" said Brown Owl. She pulled Jenna's ponytail. "You were a worry, Jenna Daylight. One of the worst scouts I ever had!"

"I can believe that," said Tom. He and Jenna laughed, and I felt left out again. I turned away.

"Well, see you tomorrow," said Mom. "Sleep well, Andy."

But as it turned out, Andy didn't sleep at all.

I went by myself to get Andy the next day.

Mom and Dad had to go out. Tom and Jenna
had disappeared somewhere. I knew Andy
and I couldn't carry all her stuff, so I took the
wheelbarrow. Darn Tom and Jenna, I
thought. Tom should have been here to help.

I glanced at the old house next to the scout cabin as I passed by. It *was* an interesting place, I thought. I'd like to have a closer look sometime.

Andy looked tired and heavy-eyed when she came out of the cabin. "Are you OK?" I asked. "Were you up giggling all night?"

"No," said Andy. "Well, not giggling. It was a little strange. I'll tell you later."

We piled Andy's stuff into the wheelbarrow. Sammy jumped onto the sleeping bag and settled himself down for a ride. Outside the old house, Andy paused. "That's what was strange," she said. "That house. Jenna said it was empty, didn't she?"

"Yes," I said. "No one's lived there for years and years, she said."

"Well," said Andy. "There were lights on in there last night."

"Lights?" I said. "Maybe someone's moved in."

"Doesn't much look like it, does it?" said Andy.

She was right. There were waist-high weeds right up to the front door.

"It does seem funny," I said. "What did everyone else think?"

"They didn't see," said Andy. "It was about midnight. Everyone else was asleep."

"Why weren't you?" I asked.

"We'd been telling ghost stories." Andy was a little embarrassed. "I couldn't go to sleep."

I knew that would be true. Andy's never really liked ghost stories.

"I could see a light sort of moving on the ceiling in our cabin," said Andy. "So I got up. And there were lights on in that house."

"Want to take a look?" I asked.

There were scouts and their parents everywhere. "Not now," Andy said. "Let's come back later."

So we did.

Chapter 2

Someone at the Window

Later that afternoon, Andy and I went back to the old house. Tom and Jenna still weren't around, so we called Sammy and went by ourselves.

We stopped on the sidewalk and looked at the old house. It looked a lot like ours had looked before Mom and Dad started working on it. The windows were cracked, the front steps were broken, and it urgently needed a coat of paint.

Andy and I started to push our way through the high weeds in the yard. Sammy sat down on the sidewalk. "Come on, Sammy!" called Andy. Sammy whined, but at last he followed her. He didn't look happy.

I reached the front steps and turned around. "What's the matter, Sammy?" I said. I tried to pat him, but Sammy backed away. He was looking up at the house, and he growled. "What's the problem, fella?" I said. Sammy growled again.

"There's someone there!" said Andy.

She was looking up at the house, too. I stepped back and looked up. And then I saw it.

The ragged remains of curtains at an upstairs window twitched, as if someone had moved them. Someone was hiding

behind them, and looking out. There was a
giggle, a whisper. The curtains twitched
again, and this time I saw a hint of a child's
face at the window. It was a girl's face.

"It's kids!" I said. "I bet someone's using the
house for a clubhouse—like they used our
house before we moved in! Come on!"

I started for the front steps, but Andy caught my arm. "Wait," she said. "I don't know . . . I don't like it."

"Don't like what?" I said. "It's just kids!"

I started up the front steps. I knew they were a bit rickety, but they didn't look too bad. Suddenly, there was a cracking sound, and then a crash. The step I'd just put my foot on fell apart right under me.

Chapter 3

No One Lives Here

I grabbed the railing, and just managed to stop myself from going down with the broken step.

"Issy! Are you OK?" shouted Andy.

"Yes," I said. "I'm fine." I was staring at the steps. It was weird, because I hadn't put my weight on the broken step at all. It had just fallen apart. "Be careful, Andy," I said. "Hold onto the railing."

Andy still wasn't happy about it, but she followed me up the steps.

Sammy wouldn't come in at all. He sat down firmly in the garden.

"Oh, all right," I said. "Wait there then." I pushed the front door. It swung back with a creak and a groan.

"Hello," I called. "Anyone here?"

"Let's go!" said Andy suddenly.

"Is anyone here?" I called again.

This time, I heard a giggle. It was a little girl's giggle.

The hall was dim after the bright sun outside. I couldn't see anything at first. Then I heard a giggle again. I looked up. Some children were standing in the hall.

There were three of them—a boy about Tom's age, a girl who might be my age,

and a very little girl, about four or five.

"Hi!" I said. "I'm Isabel. This is Andy."

I waited. The girl about my age glanced at
the boy. He folded his arms and stared at
me. The little girl smiled broadly and started
toward us. The boy tried to stop her, but he
was too late. "Hello! I'm Caroline!" she said.
"That's George, and that's Stephanie."

The boy frowned. The bigger girl bit her lip. What's wrong with them? I thought. The little girl smiled. "Come and see the house," she said.

"No!" The other girl, Stephanie, called. "Not yet, Caroline."

"You shouldn't be here," the boy, George, said. He didn't sound friendly.

"Why not?" I said. "You're here!"

Andy slid her hand into mine. "Issy, let's go," she whispered. "I don't like it here."

But I wasn't going yet. "Are you using the house for a clubhouse?" I asked Stephanie.

She looked uncertainly at George. "Yes . . . no . . . " she stammered.

I wasn't going to find out much from her. I turned to Caroline. "Do you play here?" I asked.

Caroline laughed. "I live here," she said.

"No one lives here!" said Andy.

"I do," said Caroline definitely.

"Issy, I really want to go *now*," Andy said. I was surprised. Her voice was shaking.

"OK," I said. "We'll go." I turned to the three children. "See you later," I said, and I meant it. I was coming back. That George couldn't tell *me* what to do!

Chapter 4

Names on Headstones

Andy was already outside. "I hate this place!" she said. "Those kids are weird!"

"Weird? How?" I asked.

"Well, their clothes were funny," said Andy. "Just weird!"

"Can't say I noticed," I said. "The girls were OK, but not that George!"

"I'm never going there again," said Andy.

I tried to talk Andy into taking Sammy to the old house the next day for his walk. "No way," said Andy. So I went by myself.

Sammy and I took our time. As we passed the little wooden church, Tom and Jenna rode their bikes toward me. "Where are you going?" they called.

"Just walking," I said. "Exploring."

"Have you been into the churchyard?" asked Jenna. "There are some really old graves there." She propped her bike on the fence and started pointing out the old graves to Tom. I followed, reading names on headstones as I went by. Then I stopped. Three names leaped out at me—*George, Stephanie, Caroline.*

I looked at the headstones again. George Hamilton, died 1918, age 16. Stephanie

Armstrong, died 1948, age 12. Caroline Bertoni, died 1968, age 5. I sat down on the grass with a thump.

"Issy!" said Tom. "Are you OK? You're as white as a ghost!"

"Funny you should say that," I said.

Tom and Jenna hardly believed me when I told them about the three children in the old house. "Coincidence," Tom said. But then Jenna looked thoughtful. She said she didn't know any kids in town called George, Stephanie, or Caroline.

"Then they could be . . . ghosts?" I said.

"Let's go see!" said Jenna.

We went to the old house. We went through every room.

There was no one there, no one at all. And no sign of life. Dust and cobwebs covered everything.

I could tell Tom and Jenna didn't believe I'd met three children called George, Stephanie, and Caroline—children who might be ghosts.

"It all fits," I said. "Their clothes, the names in the cemetery, the ages, are all right."

"Could still be a coincidence," said Tom.

"I don't think so," I said stubbornly.

"I'd need to see them first," said Tom.

"All right, *be* like that!" I yelled.

"Hey, chill out," said Jenna. I could see she didn't like Tom and me fighting.

"Let's go," said Tom. Jenna looked at me
uncomfortably, but they got on their bikes
and rode off. I felt really alone. Even Sammy
went with them.

Well, who needed them anyway? I thought.
I'd explore the house by myself!

As soon as I reached the door, I heard a giggle. Caroline opened the door. George and Stephanie were standing in the hall.

I spent the whole afternoon with the three children, playing jacks and dominoes and hide-and-seek. George was still standoffish. He scared me. But the girls were nice. When I left, Caroline said, "Will you come tomorrow? And the next day?"

I hesitated. What if they *were* ghosts? Did I care? Stephanie and Caroline were the first real friends I'd made for myself in this town.

"Yes," I said to Caroline. "Yes, I'll come."

And I did.

Chapter 5

A Strange Invitation

I went to the old house after school. Andy didn't like it. "They're weird!" she said.

"Who's weird?" said Tom, coming up.

"Those midnight children," said Andy. She turned away. "Tell Issy not to go there, Tom!"

"I hope you didn't tell Andy about the headstones," said Tom. "You know that would scare her."

"Get real! Of course I didn't!" I said.

But my feelings were hurt. A few months ago, Tom wouldn't have asked me a question like that.

"Andy's right," said Tom. "That place is weird. Better keep out."

"Thanks for caring," I said.

The house and the children *were* weird, I had to admit. But it's not every day you meet a ghost—and I'd met three of them!

I wanted to know more about them. So I dropped in at the old house nearly every day to see Stephanie and Caroline and George, if he was feeling sociable.

I really wanted to know what it was *like*, being a ghost. But the midnight children couldn't—or wouldn't—tell me.

If I asked about their families, or homes,

they just looked confused, and told me this was where they lived. Maybe they had all lived here, I thought. More than eighty years ago, fifty years ago, and thirty years ago. Where were their families now? Were the midnight children all alone, or were there other ghosts? I really wondered.

Then I had the chance to find out. One afternoon, Stephanie and Caroline were looking excited. They were going to have a party, they said. A party! On the fifteenth of October. Could I come? They'd really like me to come!

George wasn't saying anything. "I'd like to," I said, "but only if George wants me to come, too."

"Of course," he said slowly. "You're invited."

"Who else is coming?" I asked. But at once the midnight children got vague and confused.

"Lots of people, I think," said Caroline.

"Come and see," said George.

"All right," I said. "I will! When does it start?"

"Midnight," said George.

"That's kind of late," I started to say. Then I stopped. Midnight was just right if the other guests were ghosts. "I'll be there," I said.

Chapter 6

Searching Through the Past

I didn't mean to tell Andy about the party. I knew she'd worry. But, somehow, on the fifteenth of October, the day of the party, I let something slip. Then Andy wouldn't give up until she heard all about it.

"I don't want you to go," she said.

"Well, I'm going," I said. "A ghost party! I'm not missing that!"

Andy didn't say any more. But I found out

later that she told Tom and Jenna. They didn't like the idea either.

"I think we need to find out more about those kids," said Jenna.

"If they exist," said Tom.

"They do!" wailed Andy. "And I don't want Issy to go there!"

"OK, OK," said Tom. "But where do we find out about kids who lived years and years ago?"

"The library?" said Jenna. "They'll have a town history."

The librarian did have a town history, but the midnight children's names weren't in it.

"But if you're looking for information on people," the librarian said, "maybe you should try old newspapers. We've got them all on disk—1918, 1948, and 1968, wasn't it?"

She gave Tom and Jenna a pile of disks and a computer to work at. "Now you just have to search," she said.

They were still searching when it was time for the library to close. "But we haven't finished!" said Jenna. "And it's important!"

The librarian hesitated. "I really shouldn't," she said, "but I'll let you take the disks home. They have to be back tomorrow."

"Thanks!" said Tom. "Come on, we can work at our house."

It was a good thing Mom and Dad were out that night, I thought. Here it was eleven o'clock, and Andy was still up. She kept checking on me, to see what I was doing. Tom and Jenna were working on the computer. And I was getting ready to go to a midnight ghost party!

I didn't say anything to Tom, Jenna, or Andy.
I just quietly left the house at eleven-thirty.

I found out later that Andy went to my room
not long after I'd left. She knew right away
where I'd gone. She raced downstairs to tell
Tom and Jenna.

Tom and Jenna had just found the last piece of information they were looking for. They didn't like it at all. They checked the notes they'd made.

"George Hamilton died as the result of an accident in 1918. Stephanie Armstrong died as the result of an accident in 1948. Caroline Bertoni died as the result of an accident in 1968," said Jenna. "All of them died on the fifteenth of October!"

"No prizes for guessing where," said Tom. He looked up. Andy was behind him. "Where's Issy?" he said sharply.

Andy was staring, horrified, at their notes. "Issy's gone," she whispered.

Tom and Jenna looked at the clock. It was eleven fifty-five. Five minutes to midnight.

"Let's go!" said Tom.

Chapter 7

At Midnight

I was at the old house early. It looked dark and empty. But just before midnight, lights started going on. One room, then another, until the whole house was ablaze with light.

This was it! I took a deep breath and started up the broken steps. The door swung open. I could see George and Stephanie and Caroline, but no one else. Where were the other guests?

"Come in!" called George. I hesitated and took a deep breath. Then I walked into the hall.

As I did, Tom and Jenna and Andy ran into the yard. The midnight children moved toward the door as Tom reached the steps.

"You can't come in," said George. He sounded angry. I looked at Stephanie and Caroline. Could they be crying?

The midnight children stood in front of Tom and Jenna and Andy. "You can't stop it now," they said. "It wants her. It wants Isabel to live here, too."

"It?" shouted Tom. "What do you mean, *it?*"

"The house," the midnight children said. "The house, of course. The house wants Isabel."

"What do you mean?" yelled Jenna. And suddenly there was a creaking, cracking noise from the old house. We all looked up.

"Listen," the midnight children whispered. "Listen. It's time."

It was midnight. Right in front of our eyes the midnight children wavered, faded, and disappeared. The lights went out. In the darkness, the house cracked above me.

"Issy!" yelled Tom. "Issy!" He leaped into the hall, grabbed my arm, and pulled me toward the door.

"Run!" shouted Jenna. We all hurled ourselves across the porch, fell down the broken steps, and landed in the yard.

Inside the house, a pile of timber, glass, and iron crashed down from the roof into the hall. It landed right where I'd been standing. I felt sick. I'd nearly been under that!

"It's the *house*!" said Tom. "It was the house that got the children!"

"And it wants more," said Jenna.

We scrambled up. At the gate, we stopped and turned to look back at the old house.

The cracking sound grew louder and louder—the same sound we heard when the pile of rubble crashed down from the roof.

As we watched, the house began to shake violently, and a dull, red glow began to spread upward from its foundation.

"Look," whispered Jenna in awe. "The house is angry. It wanted Issy, and it didn't get her. Now it's throwing a temper tantrum . . . a full-blown temper tantrum."

"It's going to explode," cried Andy.

"Yes," said Tom. "People will hear the noise. They'll come to see what's happening. Let's get out of here—fast!"

Jenna led the way, and we turned to run.

Suddenly, the sound of exploding walls and collapsing timbers shattered the night. Then, silence . . . dead silence.

Tom and I stopped in our tracks. Tom put his arm around my shoulders. "Come on, Issy. It's over. It's done. We need to go."

The next day, we all went to look at the old house. There was nothing left but a heap of splintered timber and twisted metal. We turned our backs on it and went into the churchyard. Andy had brought a big bunch of flowers from our garden. Carefully she put flowers on each of three graves.

"Where do you think George and Stephanie and Caroline will go?" she asked.

We didn't know. But somehow, we felt the midnight children were very close to us. The house that had held them prisoner was gone forever. We felt the midnight children were now free and happy.

About the Author

Pamela Rushby

Pamela Rushby has worked in advertising, as a preschool teacher, and as a freelance writer. She is currently a television writer and producer.

Pamela has written over 30 books for children. She lives with her husband, two children, a three-legged cat, and six visiting wild turkeys that peck at the back door for handouts.

She is passionately interested in children's books, television, ancient history, and Middle Eastern food. Although Pamela likes writing about ghosts, she has never met one personally.

About the Illustrator

Kevin Burgemeestre

Kevin illustrates books and prepares collages for a magazine. When he illustrates with ink, Kevin uses a dip-in mapping pen in a loose, friendly manner. For his colored illustrations, he works in either watercolor with soft washes, or strong color applied with sponges. Kevin's collages reflect his passion for movies and cubism, and sometimes end up as sculptures.

Kevin works out of his own studio, which he shares with his enormous collection of car magazines, and his young son, Jim, drawing, drawing, drawing . . .